SLAVERY

AND The Civil War

SLAVERY
AND The Civil War

What your History Teacher Didn't Tell You
A Handbook to Combat Revisionist History

Garry Bowers, M. Ed.

SHOTWELL PUBLISHING
Columbia, South Carolina

Produced in the Republic of South Carolina by

Shotwell Publishing, LLC
Post Office Box 2592
Columbia, South Carolina 29202

www.ShotwellPublishing.com

Cover Design: Boo Jackson Graphic Design

ISBN: 978-1-947660-20-5

10 9 8 7 6 5 4 3 2

Dedicated to the love of my life, Linda Garvey, who was not the least bit interested in the subject matter of this work, but nevertheless encouraged and supported me to its completion, and to our grandchildren so they will not be the slaves of revisionist history.

Contents

PREFACE

THE EVENTS OF 1861-1865 which we call "the Civil War" are still the biggest thing in American history. Given the size of the population at the time, nothing since has ever equaled those years in the scale of military mobilization, the intense and bloody warfare over vast areas of our own soil, the vast destruction of life and property, and the trauma of enforced revolutionary change in society.

Our humanity cries to understand. This must have been *about* something. How can it be justified? Our understanding falls back upon romance and righteousness to avoid despair. It must have been a noble and necessary effort carried out against evil people who refused to give up their slaves.

It will help us to do something Americans seldom do and face exactly what happened. What happened was this: the party in control of the federal government, representing only two-fifths of the American people, raised an army of unprecedented size and launched an immense invasion in order to suppress the Southern States that had declared their independence. Resistance was fierce and skillful. The party in control of the government achieved victory at last by a "total war" policy against Southern civilians. The "Union" justified itself to itself and to the world by declaring the war a crusade against the great evil of slavery. This claim was made in the middle of the war and had not been previously declared.

ix

In today's America, obsessed with race and victimisation, that story is easy to sell. But is it true? Did those men in blue really sacrifice their lives for the freedom and equality of black Americans? Did those men in gray give their lives so that they could continue to hold black Americans in slavery. Garry Bowers tackles this question with learning, reason, and courage. Shotwell is proud to publish this work, which we hope will prove to be useful to teachers and students.

— The Publisher

INTRODUCTION

"The most effective way to destroy a people is to deny and obliterate their own understanding of their history."
— George Orwell

THIS TREATISE IS WRITTEN to dispel some of the frighteningly common incorrect beliefs and woefully inaccurate concepts of the greatest conflict in American history, specifically as it applies to slavery. It is written so that when the "American Civil War" is relegated to but a few paragraphs in our history books in another 150 years, someone may find this in a dusty archive and salvage from it some realistic reasoning or at least conclude that popular history may not be scrupulous history.

This little book will be deemed controversial, at best. Those who have rewritten our history, often by omission, and those who perpetuate such revision are legion. And they are powerful. They thrive in academia, Hollywood, the national electronic and print media and the halls of legislatures. They demonize entire groups of people to substantiate their elitism. They use the politics of victimization for their own selfish ends. They are the racists who use that very term to slander those with whom they disagree. They are the "progressives" who preserve myths in order to protect their pretensions and self-righteous indignation.

Those who hold up truth as more valuable than a social or political agenda may benefit from the contents herein. And if only one sentence is remembered or repeated from this labor, let it be this: One can never understand history if contemporary standards are applied to past situations.

365,000 Union soldiers did not die to abolish slavery. 258,000 Confederate soldiers did not die to support slavery. This number is the most conservative. Most sources quote more, up to one million.

I. THE CIVIL WAR THAT WASN'T

OF ALL THE MISCONCEPTIONS about the American "Civil War," perhaps the most superlative is its very name. A civil war, by denotative or connotative definition, occurs when a faction wishes to overthrow or control an existing government in order to impose its own ideology upon the governed.

The Southern states that seceded from the Union had neither the desire nor the plans to take command of the country. They simply wanted to withdraw from it, and arguably, according to even some modern constitutionalists and historians, had a right to do so, based upon the nation's origins. Virginia, New York and Rhode Island demanded that the right of secession be reserved before they would even agree to the Constitution, thereby implying that secession was indeed a right reserved by individual states.[1]

The United States had, after all, seceded from Great Britain only two generations before the states of the Confederacy did so. "When in the course of human events, it becomes necessary for one people to dissolve the political bonds which

---

[1] Dr. Ray L. Parker, "The Union Was Never in Jeopardy," *Confederate Veteran*, May/Jun 2017, pp. 10-11

1

have connected them with another..." states the beginning of the Declaration of Independence.[2] That could not have been more applicable than it was to the Southern states in 1861, as will be exhibited in the pages following.

Of the 30 or so names for the conflict, assigned both during and after the War, from both sides, there are several that describe it much more accurately than "Civil War."[3] Note that this term was used in the very title of this book, simply because it is traditional and recognizable but not because it is accurate. Had some other of the titles been used, many, if not most, people would not know to what this work referred. Hereafter, it will be referred to as "the War."

The second most common name is "The War Between the States." However, biased Northern writers and other revisionist historians, in a conscious attempt to scapegoat the South, began using the labels "slave states" for the Confederacy and "free states" for all others, ignoring the fact that up to 20% of slaves were held in the "free states," and thereby invalidating this title.

Other names include, according to one's loyalties, "The War of the Rebellion," "The War of Northern Aggression," "The War to Preserve the Union," and "The War for Southern

---

[2] Thomas Jefferson, "The unanimous Declaration of the thirteen united States of America," National Archives, https://www.archives.gov/founding-docs/declaration-transcript

[3] Paul Jordan, *The Civil War*, National Geographic Society, 1969, pp. 11-13, 18, 27, 30, 32-33, 112

Independence."[4] The last is by far the most accurate and relates the legitimate cause of the conflict.

In U.S. official government records, it is known as "The War of the Rebellion."[5] This title, too, is incorrect. In 1867, none other than U.S. Supreme Court Justice Salmon P. Chase noted, in his declaration that Jefferson Davis (or any other Confederate) could not be tried for treason, that "Secession is not rebellion." So, this label too is inaccurate.

It is also known widely as "Mr. Lincoln's War, which is not too far off base, and "The Brother's War," which sadly, is far too accurate. Our personal favorite, as a matter of classical understatement, is "The Late Unpleasantness." But regardless of the plethora of names available, it is important to note that only one very obscure and rarely used title for the most devastating event in American history even mentions slavery. It can then readily be concluded that slavery was neither the cause nor the focus of the War.

---

[4] *Ibid.*
[5] *Ibid.*

II. Red, Black, and White

IT IS IMPOSSIBLE TO FULLY COMPREHEND any subject without exploring its history. The following is a brief chronicle of slavery in the United States.

Slavery in what is now the continental United States was in existence long before Europeans set foot upon its soil. It was common practice for the Native Americans to take slaves from other tribes or even sects or villages within the same tribe. Upon capture in the commonly instigated wars, the unfortunate prisoners would be returned to the victor's town where, depending upon the prevailing conditions, they were often slowly tortured and eventually (and mercifully) killed. The more fortunate were frequently crippled to prevent their escape and enslaved for life. Some lucky few were ultimately adopted into the tribe.[6]

However, fellow Indians were not the only slaves of the Native Americans. On one of the many early Spanish expeditions into Florida, the first person they encountered was a Spaniard from a previous expedition who had been taken as a slave by the Indians. The Spanish themselves took the

---

[6] "America's Fascinating Indian Heritage," *Readers Digest*, 1978, p. 94

indigenous people as slaves as it suited their needs. DeSoto, in his circuitous and extensive route through the Southeast, took them by the hundreds.[7]

When the early French and British settlers arrived, it was common practice for the Indians to take them into bondage. Many white women and children were ransomed from the Indians by European traders from the 1600's to the 1800's.[8] As late as the 1830's, it is estimated that, of the population of Indians traveling from the Southern states to Oklahoma in the Indian Removal known as the "Trail of Tears," 25% were African and fellow Native American slaves.[9]

Into the 1800s Muslims from North Africa raided Mediterranean commerce and even the coast of Europe to seize white slaves.

Some of the first slaves in what is now the United States were white Europeans, mostly from the British Isles. In the early Colonial Period, whites were bought and sold as permanent slaves. Most think of white servitude as "indentured servants," who worked in vassalage for 3 to 7 years, usually to pay their passage to America. However, up to half of those in the New England colonies were slaves for life, as were their children. They were placed on the auction

---

[7] Albert Pickett, *Pickett's History of Alabama*, 1851
[8] *Ibid.*
[9] Senator Charles Davison, State of Alabama Senate Speech, Transcript, Confederate Heritage Fund (Andalusia, AL), 1997

block and sold just like their black counterparts, who also were found in New England.[10]

It was a black slave master named Anthony Johnson who was responsible for legalising the lifetime slavery of blacks. He won a lawsuit in Virginia courts in 1653 that changed "temporary servitude" to "lifetime servitude" for those in that category.[11]

Before the War, many whites, especially the Irish, were kidnapped by slavers or shanghaied by merchant mariners and sold to Northern white factory owners. Those who labored in such industries were almost exclusively white. Many were children. This practice continued well into the Industrial Revolution.[12]

These whites were purchased by the Industrial magnates at a much cheaper rate than blacks for two reasons. Transport was not as expensive because most were captured in Ireland, and they did not have to purchase them from the slave masters of Africa. Both the British and the Americans considered the Irish no better than the Africans, and sometimes they sold for produce rather than money.[13]

In the South those white slaves who had migrated, through sale or barter, were considered more lowly than the blacks.

---

[10] "Indentured Servitude," Wikipedia, n.d

[11] Davison, State of Alabama Senate Speech.

[12] Daniel Deville, "White Slavery in America," VN Forum, September 5, 2008, https://www.vnnforum.com/showthread.php?t=79466

[13] *Ibid.*

Because blacks were worth more monetarily than the Irish, it was common for the whites to be placed in the cargo holds of riverboats unloading cotton or in the bottom of wells being constructed because those were the most dangerous positions.[14] In 1830, the Reverend Richard Oastler attacked the hypocrisy of people who condemned black slavery and ignored the plight of the white slaves who labored in Northern factories in conditions much more horrid than that which the black slaves of the agrarian South faced.[15]

Black slavery existed in North America from its early settlements and increased proportionately as the population grew, particularly after the American Revolution. United States slave ships sailing from Massachusetts, Rhode Island, and New York were financed by New England profiteers who grew rich on the trade.[16] Until the foreign slave trade (not slave ownership) was outlawed in 1808, it was big business in the Northeastern states. Foreign ships bringing slaves to our shores primarily flew the flags of France, Spain, Portugal and Britain.[17]

Nigeria was one of the largest slave holding nations in the world during this time and was the largest single source of black slaves in America.[18] Slavers bought this human cargo

---

[14] *Ibid.*
[15] *Ibid.*
[16] Davison, State of Alabama Senate Speech
[17] *Ibid.*
[18] *Ibid.*

from black slave masters.[19] Americans and Europeans did not go out into the jungles and plains of Africa to capture slaves. The dangers of disease, a hostile environment and native attack would have made such an endeavor foolhardy indeed and likely fatal.   They merely paid for the slaves at predetermined coastal locations and rowed them to the transport ships in longboats.[20]

Conditions aboard those ships during the voyage were extremely harsh. Up to 20% died during transport. However, the cruel mistreatment by their black masters prior to purchase without doubt increased their mortality rate. Many were already in the final stages of starvation and riddled with disease when they were picked up.[21]

Only 5% of African slaves were shipped to the United States.[22] The rest were sold in South America, the Spanish Empire, and the West Indies colonies of the British, French, Dutch and Danish.[23] The world prior to and long after the War was rife with slaves and slavery. It lasted well into the 20th century and still thrives in various forms in a multitude of places, especially Africa.

---

[19] Pickett, *Pickett's History of Alabama*
[20] Davison, State of Alabama Senate Speech
[21] *Ibid.*
[22] *Ibid.*
[23] "Abraham Lincoln — An Illustrated History of His Life and Times," *Time Magazine*, 2009, pp. 58-61, 88-89, 94

African slaves in America at the time of the War were dispersed mainly in 11 states that eventually seceded from the Union, plus Missouri, Kentucky, Delaware and Maryland. The nation's capitol, Washington D.C., had 3,185 slaves counted during the 1860 census, one year before the War.[24]

Black slavery in the continental United States existed only a little over 4 years under the Confederacy and even that was simultaneous with Union slavery. Previously, it had existed over 80 years under the Stars and Stripes, and before that, over 150 years under the flags of Europe. Slavery was fully supported by the nation's laws and courts during that time.

Though it is difficult for 21st century Americans to comprehend, the citizens living in the United States of America 150 years ago had never known life without the "peculiar institution" of slavery.[25]

---

[24] *Ibid.*

[25] William C. Davis and Bell I. Wiley, *Civil War – A Complete Photographic History*, New York: Tess Press, 2000, pp. 8, 370-376, 382, 430, 578, 815, 888; Jordan, *The Civil War*, pp. 11-13, 18, 27, 30, 32-33, 112

III. LINCOLN – THE GREAT EMANCIPATOR WHO WASN'T

LET IT BE UNEQUIVOCALLY said of Abraham Lincoln that he detested slavery on moral grounds.[26] Let it also be said that he did not send Federal troops into the South to free the slaves, but to preserve the Union. Further, if he were alive today, he would be considered the vilest of racists. Modern political correctness notwithstanding, he held most of the attitudes common in his day.[27]

Lincoln was not an abolitionist. Lincoln held no animosity toward the slaveholders. Though he "could not remember a time" when he did not "abhor the idea of slavery," he found the Northern abolitionists to be "extreme, self-righteous, and unrealistic in underestimating the difficulties that would ensue were slavery to be abolished."[28] Further, he did not

---

[26] Stephen T. Foster, *Lincoln On Slavery-A Moral Wrong, But...*, Atlas Editions, n.d.

[27] "Abraham Lincoln — An Illustrated History of His Life and Times," pp. 58-61, 88-89, 94

[28] *Ibid.*

denounce the slaveholders. "I will surely not blame them for not doing what I should not know how to do myself."[29]

In fact, Lincoln said of the slave owners, "if slavery did not exist among them, they would not introduce it. If it did now exist among us, we should not instantly give it up."[30] These are not the words of a man who invaded the Southern states in order to free the slaves or punish the slave owners.

As munificent as his philosophy was toward slave owners, Lincoln held no such feelings toward the Negro. Aside from the slaves of his wife's family (who were, incidentally, her slaves by familial tradition) he had little contact with the Black race. He spoke of the Todd slaves as being treated "in a paternalistic fashion,"[31] as indeed a great majority of slaves were treated.

He did meet and talk to ex-slave and activist Frederick Douglass once. However, that was of political motivation, to organize a band of Black spies. Lincoln had no Black friends.[32] And he met with a delegation of Blacks in 1862 and urged them to emigrate to Central America, telling them, "You are far removed from being placed on an equality with the White race."[33]

---

[29] Jordan, *The Civil War*, pp. 11-13, 18, 27, 30, 32-33, 112

[30] Foster, *Lincoln On Slavery*

[31] "Abraham Lincoln—An Illustrated History of His Life and Times," pp. 58-61, 88-89, 94

[32] *Ibid.*

[33] *Ibid.*

More than two years before the war, he summed up his feelings regarding the Black race. In the 1858 debate with Stephen Douglas, Lincoln stated, "I will say then, that I am not, nor ever have been, in favor of bringing about in any way the social and political equality of the Black and White races. That I am not nor ever have been in favor of making voters or jurors of Negroes nor of qualifying them to hold office, nor to intermarry with White people and I will say in addition to this that there is a physical difference between the White and Black races. I, as much as any other man, am in favor of having the superior position assigned to the White race."[34] He later stated, "What then? Free them and make them our own political and social equals? My own feeling would not admit of this!"[35]

Lincoln's lack of admiration for those enslaved did not end there. Not only did he think they should not be equal citizens, he wished them removed from the United States. "My first impulse would be to free all the slaves and send them to Liberia."[36] On December 3, 1861 (nine months into the War), Lincoln urged Congress to appropriate money for the deportation of Blacks. At that time, he preferred either Liberia or Central America as their ultimate destination.[37]

---

[34] Col. John Napier, "Warriors," Montgomery Advertiser, 1861 (Reprinted in Capitol Confederate Newsletter, 1996)

[35] Foster, Lincoln On Slavery

[36] Ibid.

[37] Ibid.; "Abraham Lincoln — An Illustrated History of His Life and Times," pp. 58-61, 88-89, 94

As late as 1863, Lincoln had not given up on his deportation plan. Though General Ulysses S. Grant had wanted to militarily take over the Dominican Republic and send them all there,[38] Lincoln followed through with his plan of removal on an experimental basis and sent 450 Black freedmen to Haiti. Almost half died of smallpox and starvation.[39]

There can be no question that his purpose in the War was definitely not to free the slaves. In his Inaugural Speech on March 4, 1861, the new President said, "I have no purpose, directly or indirectly, to interfere with the institution of slavery. I believe I have no lawful right to do so and I have no inclination to do so."[40]

Immediately following secession, Lincoln and the U.S. Congress offered the South the Corwin Amendment which, among other things, guaranteed permanent slavery forever in the seceding states if only they would return to the Union.[41] Three states had already ratified the amendment when Ft. Sumter was fired upon and approval became moot.[42]

----

[38] Dan McLaughlin, "Rethinking President Grant (Part Two)," *National Review*, February 26, 2019, https://www.nationalreview.com/2019/02/ulysses-grant-presidency-economy-corruption-foreign-policy/
[39] Davis and Wiley, *Civil War – A Complete Photographic History*, pp. 8, 370-376, 382, 430, 578, 815, 888
[40] Davison, State of Alabama Senate Speech
[41] Richard Marksburg, "Culture Wars and Revisionist History," *Confederate Veteran*, Jul/Aug 2016, pp. 20, 26-29
[42] Davison, State of Alabama Senate Speech

When the War began, the U.S. House of Representatives overwhelmingly passed a resolution, with which Lincoln agreed, declaring the purpose of the conflict. Not only did this document not even mention "slavery" as a cause, it asserted that slavery would be preserved should the North win and the Union be reunited.[43] In light of such events, it is patently absurd to assume the North invaded the South to free the slaves.

Further, if the War had been initiated to end slavery, Lincoln would not have waited almost two years to issue the Emancipation Proclamation. It is quite apparent that this motive was added ex post facto to conceal the real reason for the North's invasion: economic hegemony.

In the first year of the War, U.S. General John Fremont took it upon himself to free the slaves of Confederate sympathizers in the border state of Missouri. Lincoln modified the order to comply with the Confiscation Act, by which troops could only seize slaves actually used "in aid of the rebellion." His concern then was not emancipation, but the continued loyalty of the Border states.[44]

The Department of the South, a Union military command led by David Hunter, declared in 1862 that the slaves of South Carolina, Georgia and Florida be "forever free." Upon

---

[43] Marksburg, "Culture Wars and Revisionist History," pp. 20, 26-29

[44] Davis and Wiley, *Civil War – A Complete Photographic History*, pp. 8, 370-376, 382, 430, 578, 815, 888

learning of this, Lincoln declared that pronouncement "altogether void" and rescinded the order, though it was basically the same as the Emancipation Proclamation that would be issued the following year.[45] Hunter then formed a regiment of fugitive slaves. Lincoln and the War Department refused to commission or pay for the Black soldiers. Hunter returned them to their owners.[46]

Lincoln then went on to fire Secretary of War Cameron primarily because he advocated making soldiers of Negroes.[47] It wasn't until the issuance of the Emancipation Proclamation in 1863 that Lincoln gave approval for the use of "colored soldiers." That was, like the Proclamation itself, a matter of politics and expediency, for he stated that "slavery enables the enemies of free institutions to taunt us as hypocrites."[48] It was not his love for Blacks or even his opposition to slavery that was important, but the perception of other countries that were leaning toward support for the South.

Perhaps the most definitive statement Lincoln made concerning slavery's connection with the War came in an interview with the famous journalist Horace Greeley, two years after the conflict had begun. "My paramount object in this struggle is to save the Union and it is not to save or destroy

---

[45] *Ibid.*
[46] *Ibid.*
[47] *Ibid.*
[48] Foster, *Lincoln On Slavery*; Jordan, *The Civil War*, pp. 11-13, 18, 27, 30, 32-33, 112

slavery." He went on to say that if he could only save the Union by keeping slavery, he would do so.[49] This War was not about freeing the slaves.

---

[49] Parker, "The Union Was Never in Jeopardy," pp. 10-11

IV. THE EMANCIPATION PROCLAMATION THAT DIDN'T

THE EMANCIPATION PROCLAMATION was not an altruistic document. It did not free anyone. It did not free the slaves in the Southern states to which it was directed because the federal government had no control over those states.[50] It did not even attempt to free the approximately one-half million* slaves held in the Northern states. Those remained slaves throughout the War.[51] In 1861, bills that called for a referendum in the capital city to pay slave owners there to free their slaves failed miserably.[52]

In the first year of the War, Congress, even though made up only of Northern senators and representatives, refused to pass a constitutional amendment abolishing slavery in Washington. The Emancipation Proclamation neither offered citizenship for the slaves nor did it offer to compensate their

---

[50] Abraham Lincoln, "Emancipation Proclamation" (1863), National Archives, https://www.archives.gov/exhibits/featured-documents/emancipation-proclamation/transcript.html

[51] Foster, *Lincoln On Slavery*

[52] "Ending Slavery in the District of Columbia," DC.gov, n.d., www.emancipation.dc.gov/page/ending-slavery-district-columbia

owners for financial loss as required by the 5th amendment to the Constitution.[53]

The Emancipation Proclamation was issued for two reasons. Primarily, it was a propaganda weapon. After two years of Confederate land victories, Europe began to see the South as a viable, legitimate nation, with whom they could trade at a 10% tariff instead of the exorbitant rate offered by the Union.[54] The Proclamation served notice to those foreign powers that the Confederacy might not be a stable trading partner if slave labor were eradicated.

Lincoln and Secretary of State Seward decided to issue the Proclamation in 1863 because they had just had their first major Union victory: Antietam. Most scholars hardly classify that battle as a Union victory.[55] It was the bloodiest day of the War to that point. The North lost 12,000 men and the South lost 10,500. Either Lincoln and Seward believed the wholly incorrect propaganda coming from Northern newspapers or they agreed it was as close as they had come to a victory. The Proclamation was issued on the heels of that battle so the document would not be construed as a desperate gamble by the losing side.[56]

---

[53] John Sophocleus, "Emancipation Proclamation Sesquicentennial," *Alabama Gazette*, January 2013, pp. 14-15

[54] *Ibid.*

[55] John Zwemer, *Civil War Trivia*, Sweetwater Press, 2006, pp. 54, 58, 61, 111, 103-10

[56] Sophocleus, "Emancipation Proclamation Sesquicentennial," pp. 14-15

The second reason for the issuance of the Proclamation is obviously its use as a military stratagem. That failed miserably. It was believed that if they could eliminate essential workers, the South's economy and war machine would crumble. However, the expected slave rebellion never came. That should have been no surprise.

Slaves could have ended the War in the first few months of invasion had they chosen to do so. They did not, bringing about an embarrassing dilemma for Lincoln. Perhaps slavery was not the evil, oppressive institution it was supposed to be if its victims chose not to rise up, especially with their overwhelming numbers and the official support of the Emancipation Proclamation.

Further, the document almost caused mutiny and did cause large scale desertion among many units of Federal soldiers. Some generals were themselves horrified at the very idea.[57] Only the firm persuasion by field officers kept many military units from disintegrating. Ulysses S. Grant himself said, "If I thought this war was to abolish slavery, I would resign my commission and offer my sword to the other side."[58]

[57] "Abraham Lincoln — An Illustrated History of His Life and Times," pp. 58-61, 88-89, 94
[58] Davison, State of Alabama Senate Speech

V. BLACK

THE PREVAILING MODERN perception of slaves and slavery, born, as noted earlier, of progressive politics, distorted entertainment, and politically correct propagandistic history books, is one in which sadistic white overseers with bullwhips roamed large Southern cotton plantations routinely and indiscriminately beating ragged, starved and overworked Blacks into submission. A South covered by huge cotton plantations like "Tara" in *Gone With the Wind* is utter myth, and fiction as reality is dangerous. Harriet Beecher Stowe's *Uncle Tom's Cabin* stirred a firestorm of hatred for the South in the Northern states.[59] Ms. Stowe had never even visited the South or met a slave there.[60]

Only 15 people in the United States owned more than 500 slaves. Less than 1% of slave owners owned anywhere near 100 slaves.[61] A huge majority of the 7% of the population who owned slaves had between 4 and 5.[62] This is about the same number of family members of the owner for whom they

---

[59] Davison, State of Alabama Senate Speech

[60] Jordan, *The Civil War*, pp. 11-13, 18, 27, 30, 32-33, 112

[61] "Abraham Lincoln — An Illustrated History of His Life and Times," pp. 58-61, 88-89, 94

[62] *Ibid.*; Davison, State of Alabama Senate Speech

worked.[63] Incidentally, there were over 250,000 free Blacks living in the South during the 1860 census and they owned over 60,000 Black slaves.[64]

Most slaves were owned by small farmers and small business proprietors. They worked vegetable and tobacco farms, sawmills and cattle and horse ranches. They worked in carpentry and masonry enterprises or were involved with textile production or boat building or barrel making. They worked as wainwrights and blacksmiths and mechanics. Only a tiny minority worked on the sprawling storied cotton plantations.[65]

Most slaves and owners worked and lived side by side. Their families cared for each other's sick and elderly. Their children played together. They worshipped together.[66] They hunted and fished together. Their lives were intertwined, as is the case with most working and living relationships.[67]

Evidence of such bonds between the families of slaves and owners are found in the letters sent home by Confederate soldiers whose families owned slaves, inquiring as the health and well being of those slaves, be they boyhood friends or "nannies" or the elderly "aunts" and "uncles." Typical were

---

[63] Jordan, *The Civil War*, pp. 11-13, 18, 27, 30, 32-33, 112

[64] Davison, State of Alabama Senate Speech

[65] "Abraham Lincoln — An Illustrated History of His Life and Times," pp. 58-61, 88-89, 94

[66] Bell Irving Wiley, *Embattled Confederates*, New York: Bonanza Books, 1964, pp. 6, 65, 77, 191-192, 231-238, 240-244, 247

[67] Davison, State of Alabama Senate Speech

those sent by Captain Henry Morrison of the 4th Virginia Infantry, who ended his letters: "Remember me affectionately to all at home, black and white."[68] And the feelings were mutual. A married slave couple said of Captain William Baldwin, killed at the Battle of Franklin, "We loved him from birth and know well that he loved us."[69]

Though there were instances of abuse and maltreatment of slaves, the idea of habitual cruelty, even on the large plantations, is absurd in the extreme. In 1850, the price (in today's currency) of a field hand was between $13,000 and $20,000.[70] Common sense demands that a successful agrarian entrepreneur would not randomly or persistently harm such an expensive investment and render him or her incapable of production. And there were numerous laws in all states of the Old South that protected slaves from abuse and there are indications that those laws were enforced.[71] They were similar to the domestic violence and child and elder abuse laws of today.

Because of the ratio of black to white, the typical master would prudently wish to keep his slaves relatively happy. The very ugly idea of insurrection was always there.[72] In the 11

---

[68] Annette Tapert, *The Brother's War*, Random House, 1988, pp. 99, 117, 130-131, 137, 191, 210-212, 229

[69] Napier, "Warriors"

[70] Jordan, The Civil War, pp. 11-13, 18, 27, 30, 32-33, 112

[71] "Slave Codes," Wikipedia, n.d., https://en.wikipedia.org/wiki/Slave_codes

[72] Davis and Wiley, *Civil War – A Complete Photographic History*, pp. 8, 370-376,

states that seceded, there were 4 million Negroes and about 5 million whites. In the Nat Turner Rebellion of 1831, about 70 slaves murdered about 60 white men, women and children almost overnight.[73]   A widespread revolt could have decimated the white population.   As a matter of fact, insurrection is exactly what the abolitionists predicted would happen.   It did not.

Many refrained from armed revolt out of genuine concern for and fidelity to their master and his family.[74] Mary Boykin Chesnut wrote, "There seems to be not a single case of a negro who betrayed his master" in war torn South Carolina.[75] Many plantations used slaves as captains and overseers.[76] These same slaves were in charge of the farms and businesses while their owners were away at war and protected the families left behind.[77] There are documented cases in which they took up arms against Union soldiers and Confederate "stragglers" to protect those families. Many times they hid the families and stood guard for their protection.[78]

382, 430, 578, 815, 888

[73] Jordan, *The Civil War*, pp. 11-13, 18, 27, 30, 32-33, 112

[74] Davis and Wiley, *Civil War – A Complete Photographic History*, pp. 8, 370-376, 382, 430, 578, 815, 888

[75] *Ibid.*

[76] *Ibid.*

[77] Davison, State of Alabama Senate Speech

[78] Davis and Wiley, *Civil War – A Complete Photographic History*, pp. 8, 370-376, 382, 430, 578, 815, 888

This care and consideration worked both ways. Slave owners often vehemently protested, both verbally and in letters to army commanders and government officials, when Confederate military units impressed their slaves to work, most often citing concerns for the slaves' health, welfare, and safety.[79]

Another reason for the absence of insurrection was the conditions in the "runaway camps" used for ex-slaves after Union forces had permanently occupied their territory. These settlements were created by the Federal government, but the misery, starvation and disease found in them was so horrendous that Northern soldiers predicted "the demise of the entire race."[80] After liberation, many slaves simply stayed where they were and continued to work.

Finally, insurrection did not come because there was no need to rebel, no matter who won the War. As one old Negro philosophically opined, "If so be it we are to get free, we get it anyhow...If we run away, where is we?"[81]

In a U.S. Government WPA survey of former slaves a great majority reported experiences that were positive relative to their treatment, care and welfare. "Concerning food, clothing and shelter," the report stated, "Southern slaves were significantly better off than their white counterparts working

---

[79] *Ibid.*

[80] Tapert, *The Brother's War*, pp. 99, 117, 130-131, 137, 191, 210-212, 229

[81] Davis and Wiley, *Civil War – A Complete Photographic History*, pp. 8, 370-376, 382, 430, 578, 815, 888

in Northern factories."[82] With no labor laws to protect them and no administrators who cared, many whites in the North, including innumerable children, worked in horrible and dangerous conditions, often 16 hours a day, 7 days a week.[83] They labored in sweatshops and factories and slept in polluted conditions for literally pennies a day.[84]

The caloric intake of pre-War slaves, according to medical studies, exceeded the caloric intake of the median U.S. population 15 years after the war. It even exceeded the U.S. "recommended daily levels of chief nutrients" in 1964. That's 1964.[85] One only need look at the multitudinous period photographs to see that slaves, for the most part, were healthy and well fed.

From those same photos, it is obvious they had suitable, though modest, housing and were decently clothed. Late in the War, they were often better dressed than the families of their owners, who had given them their hand-me-downs, which the slaves had worn only on Sundays and were thus preserved from wear.[86]

It cannot and should not be denied that there were cases of inexcusable mistreatment of some slaves. There are a few very rare photographs of whip-scarred Negroes and these were

---

[82] Davison, State of Alabama Senate Speech
[83] Deville, "White Slavery in America"
[84] Davison, State of Alabama Senate Speech
[85] *Ibid.*
[86] Wiley, *Embattled Confederates*, pp. 6, 65, 77, 191-192, 231-238, 240-244, 247

used repeatedly by the abolitionists for propaganda purposes.[87] In at least two cases, the same subject was photographed from several different angles to make it appear there were several people involved. Modern day propagandists use these same tricks.

Thankfully, this mistreatment was exceptionally uncommon. However, the slaves' dissatisfaction with their plight must not be overlooked. Some were comfortable with their lot. Some were not.[88] Though the circumstances of the slave was not nearly as dire as has been portrayed for the imagination of contemporary society, that in no way lessens the tragedy of human bondage.

It should be noted that slavery did not end in the world or even in America as, unbelievably, the naïve and gullible contend. Slavery and the slave trade continued globally well into the 20th century and exist to this day, especially in Africa. In America, it changed from chattel slavery to share-cropper slavery and affected both the black and white Southerner.

Because Sherman and many other Union generals practiced "total war,", a concept of destruction the Nazis would use 80 years later, the civilian economic infrastructure in the South was almost eradicated. Further, the policies of Federal "Reconstruction" made it impossible for the South to recover.

---

[87] Davis and Wiley, *Civil War – A Complete Photographic History*, pp. 8, 370-376, 382, 430, 578, 815, 888

[88] Wiley, *Embattled Confederates*, pp. 6, 65, 77, 191-192, 231-238, 240-244, 247

Tenant slavery, commonly called "sharecropping," was the only alternative to starvation for many immediately following the War.[89]

Over 4 million slaves, emancipated in December of 1865, were guaranteed impoverishment. The chattel system, under which they had been fed, clothed, sheltered and medically treated, was gone. The Federal government could not, and in many cases did not even try, to reproduce that care. And there were few jobs available.

There were hundreds of thousands of Southern whites rendered homeless at the end of the War. They too were jobless. With the economic policies forced upon them by their Union conquerors, that number soon grew into the millions. So, they, and the newly freed slaves, had no choice but to turn to sharecropping.[90]

Simply put, sharecropping was purposeful and insidious post-War slavery. Northern profiteers purchased huge expanses of Southern land for back taxes and the poor, which were a preponderance of the Southern population, had little choice but to farm that land for the landowners. Some Southern landowners were themselves impoverished by debt to Northern capitalists. The methodology was elemental. A family was given a shack in which to live and a "share" of the

---

[89] James Ronald Kennedy, "Sharecropping and Northern Imposed Postwar Slavery," *Confederate Veteran*, Jan/Feb 2016, pp. 11, 16-19, 56-63
[90] *Ibid.*

profits in return for planting, cultivating and harvesting a crop, most often cotton.[91]

This system of peonage lasted until World War II. There were 8 million sharecroppers by the 1930's, divided about equally between blacks and whites. It is estimated that 750,000 of them died as a direct result of the extreme labor and the poverty which attended it. They worked all year on land they did not own and lived in hovels they did not own and paid their meager profits to the creditors which had allowed them to survive the year. In a good cycle, they made 40 cents a day. In a bad one, they lost 25 cents a day. And their Northern masters made money every year and had no obligation to them whatsoever.[92]

Globally, in the middle of the 20th century, slavery abounded in the work camps, concentration camps and gulags of Mao, Hitler, Stalin and Hirohito. In the late 20th century, slavery continued in the mines and industries of Africa and South America. Chad did not even outlaw slavery until 1976. Today, it flourishes in Southeast Asia, Africa and "closed" countries like North Korea. And it exists openly in most Islamic countries. Ironically, Nigeria, the major source of African slaves in the U.S. in the 19th century, is still deeply involved in the slave trade.

---

[91] *Ibid.*
[92] *Ibid.*

Slavery has existed since civilization began. Everyone reading this, regardless of your race, ethnicity, religion or country of origin, had ancestors who were slaves.[93] It may never end.

---

[93] Davison, State of Alabama Senate Speech

VI. BLACK AND GRAY

AS PREVIOUSLY NOTED, it is glaringly apparent that the eleven states of the Confederacy did not secede from the Union in order to retain the institution of slavery. Why, then, did they secede? The answer is multifaceted: unfair tariffs; political power; cultural conflicts; distrust; divergent concepts of the roles of federal and state governments, and fear of the eventual downfall of the South's economy. [94]

George Washington recognized the differences in North and South in religion, politics and social organization in 1796. He spoke of the possibility of the destruction of the Union because of these differences 65 years before the war.[95] Thomas Jefferson wrote in 1798 that the South was completely under the saddle of Massachusetts and Connecticut and "they ride us very hard, cruelly insulting our feelings and exhausting our strength and substance."[96]

The cries for disunion were not sudden. And they were predicted from the very beginning of the Union. Like most of

---

[94] Davison, State of Alabama Senate Speech; Jordan, *The Civil War*, pp. 11-13, 18, 27, 30, 32-33, 112

[95] Marksburg, "Culture Wars and Revisionist History," pp. 20, 26-29

[96] *Ibid.*

the battles of the War, they built slowly toward eruption. In 1820, the Missouri Compromise prohibited slavery north of Missouri's southern border.[97] In 1832 South Carolina passed an ordinance nullifying federal tariffs because those tariffs favored the Northern factory owners. In 1849, California wanted to enter the Union as a "free" state, thereby upsetting the senatorial balance of power which gave the South an equal economic footing in Washington.[98]

The Kansas-Nebraska Act of 1854 struck down the Missouri Compromise and theoretically opened up more of the West to slavery.[99] The Republican Party of Lincoln immediately began to fight for repeal of that law. Note that they were not attempting to abolish slavery, but to create a situation in which they would retain Congressional power and economic gain favorable to the North. They also wanted to keep black people out of the territories, preserving them for white labour.

In 1859, John Brown, a radical abolitionist, attempted to foment a nationwide slave rebellion when he captured the arsenal at Harper's Ferry, Virginia. Brown was a murderer, an unrepentant criminal who had been raiding in the West and killing Southern citizens and their families. This gave rise to in-kind response, resulting in Missouri's neighbor being given the unenviable name of "Bleeding Kansas." The slaves did not arise to assist Brown as he predicted. He was captured and

[97] Jordan, *The Civil War*, pp. 11-13, 18, 27, 30, 32-33, 112
[98] *Ibid.*
[99] *Ibid.*

hanged.[100]   It is little wonder that Lincoln disfavored abolitionists, who labeled Brown a hero and martyr.[101]

Despite his anti-abolitionist stance, the election of Lincoln in 1860 (by less than 40% of the vote) was the proverbial final straw for the South.[102]   His victory ensured two things the South could not abide: the probability of the loss of Congressional power and, more importantly, the rise in taxes which was sure to come.

The South was agrarian and the North industrial.   With such contrasting economies, the South was already at a disadvantage.[103]   To further exacerbate the situation, Southerners sold their goods to Europe in a free market, but were forced to purchase Northern manufactured goods in a protected market, losing millions in the process. The South was being treated as an agricultural colony, forced to pay tariffs amounting to 75% of the money necessary to operate the entire federal government, but getting little to nothing in return.[104]

The financial extortion of the South and the perceived annihilation of the Northern economy without the South was the primary cause of the War. If the North were not able

---

[100] *Ibid.*

[101] *Ibid.*; Wiley, *Embattled Confederates*, pp. 6, 65, 77, 191-192, 231-238, 240-244, 247

[102] Davison, State of Alabama Senate Speech

[103] Jordan, *The Civil War*, pp. 11-13, 18, 27, 30, 32-33, 112

[104] James W. King, "Lee and Jackson Were Great Americans," *Confederate Veteran*, Mar/Apr 2016, pp. 6-7.

effectively to tax the immense Southern exports of cotton, tobacco, and rice, they would lose three quarters of their economy. The South had little choice but to secede to survive and the North had little choice but to keep them in the Union or go broke. There can be little doubt that Northern greed was primarily responsible for the War.[105]

Northern politicians consistently attempted to increase federal taxes on material bought by the South. The states which later were to become the Confederacy bought many goods from England and France because they were cheaper. Then the U.S. government passed a tariff on European imports, and the South suffered more.

Though the Constitution provided that taxes be levied uniformly throughout the states, this provision was ignored.[106] It was the objective of Lincoln and the Republicans to raise the tariff yet again.[107] His election assured that would be accomplished and indeed it was. The Morrill Tariff, the highest in history, more than doubled the import tax, which was enough to bankrupt many Southerners. It became law in March of 1861.[108] Ft. Sumter was fired upon in April of 1861.

---

[105] Tom Root, "Admiral Semmes and Those People," *Confederate Veteran*, Mar/Apr 2016, pp. 22, 26

[106] Davison, State of Alabama Senate Speech

[107] Sophocleus, "Emancipation Proclamation Sesquicentennial," pp. 14-15

[108] Gene Kizer, Jr., "The Absurdity of Slavery as a Cause of the War," *Confederate Veteran*, Mar/Apr 2017, pp. 17-18

More than any other cause, the threat of this tax had been the final catalyst for secession.[109]

Lincoln's election practically ensured the South would lose power in Congress. He and his party adamantly opposed the extension of slavery. Without new states to vote with them, the South would become politically impotent, unable to protect its economic interests or repeal the wholly unfair taxes to which it was already subject.

The South was already losing representatives every decade due to the increasingly lopsided population (22 million in the North and 5 million in the South).[110] This was especially due to large scale immigration from Germany and Ireland into the North. Without equity in the Senate, the diminishing political power of the South would continue to erode.

Further, and again in direct defiance of the law (this time a Supreme Court decision),[111] some Northern states, supported by Lincoln and his party, passed laws obstructing the recovery of fugitive slaves. They also made it clear that slave owners would be unable to carry their slaves into territories that would eventually become states. It was, then, the beginning of the end for the institution upon which the security and the self-preservation of the South depended. Not lost in all this is the irony, indeed hypocrisy, of the North wanting to destroy

---

[109] Davison, State of Alabama Senate Speech
[110] Wiley, *Embattled Confederates*, pp. 6, 65, 77, 191-192, 231-238, 240-244, 247
[111] Jordan, *The Civil War*, pp. 11-13, 18, 27, 30, 32-33, 112

the very means with which the South was providing them with money and power.

It is asinine to think, as some Southern critics do, that the lack of slave expansion was the reason for the War. When the South seceded, expansion became a moot point, for they would have no control over the states outside the boundaries of the Confederacy. Had they remained in the Union, there was at least a chance for future states to vote with them.

People of the South, being much more rural, were naturally drawn to individualism, and consequently, local governance. The growing federal bureaucracy, which would obviously only increase under Lincoln, was anathema to them. For most Southerners, the United States was perceived as a loose confederation of societies, each of which had the power to rule itself, as the Constitution intended.

Even the anti-slavery societies of the South, and there were many at first, [112] agreed that emancipation should be achieved through the individual states, not the federal government, whose growth and power were feared by a majority of Southerners.[113] James Hunter, a Tennessee cavalryman, put it concisely. He wrote that the creation of a central power "would be the very thing to guard against." He and virtually all Southerners feared the large government favored by Lincoln and considered the people of each state to be

---

[112] Sophocleus, "Emancipation Proclamation Sesquicentennial," pp. 14-15
[113] Davison, State of Alabama Senate Speech

sovereign unto themselves, and the Union to be held together by mutual compact.[114]

It is important to recall that the Revolutionary War was fought by the fathers and grandfathers of these men. They philosophically maintained that secession was a Constitutional right, as their ancestors only two generations removed had seceded from Britain and King George. They utilized that self-same idea of threats to their right of self-government as justification..[115]

It is also noteworthy that during the original ratification of the Constitution, several states declared that they reserved the right of secession. They were assured that such was presupposed.

Charles Dickens, the celebrated English writer, wrote: "Every year, as 1861 drew nearer, Southern states declared that they would submit to this [economic] extortion only while they had not the strength to resist."[116] After the issuance of the Emancipation Proclamation, when Republicans first began to use "slavery" as an excuse for the War, Dickens wrote, "The Northern onslaught against slavery is a specious piece of humbug designed to mask their desire for economic control of the Southern states."[117]

---

[114] Tapert, *The Brother's War*, pp. 99, 117, 130-131, 137, 191, 210-212, 229
[115] Davison, State of Alabama Senate Speech
[116] Sophocleus, "Emancipation Proclamation Sesquicentennial," pp. 14-15
[117] *Ibid.*

Slavery was, at most, but a peripheral, long range issue of secession for the South. It is obvious that neither the retention nor expansion of slavery was the object. Even Confederate President Jefferson Davis, in his most prominent speeches and letters, did not mention slavery. One would think that the leader of the "slave states" would complain bitterly and vehemently if abolition was a cause against which to fight. But Davis spoke only of sectional discrimination, disrespected Constitutional rights and the trampling of state governments by an overwhelming Federal government.[118]

Correspondingly, on the eve of war, Lincoln was not concerned with the issue of slavery. In the weeks leading up to his invasion of the South, Lincoln held many meetings with both groups and individuals from both the Union and the South, presumably to stop secession and prevent conflict. In none of those conferences was the subject of slavery ever broached. Lincoln only spoke repeatedly of the revenue he would lose were the Southern states to depart. Tariffs favoring the North were responsible for a great majority of the income necessary for the operation of the Federal government.[119]

Lincoln did not initiate war with the Confederacy to free the slaves. America was deep into the War before the Republicans even brought the subject up. Britain began to feel the pinch of a cotton shortage and the Union needed a cause more noble

---

[118] Marksburg, "Culture Wars and Revisionist History," pp. 20, 26-29

[119] John M. Taylor, "Union at All Costs," *Confederate Veteran*, Jan/Feb 2017, pp. 21-23

than politics and money to diminish growing support for the South.[120]   Slavery was nothing more than a convenient propaganda tool. The assurance of European neutrality was a necessity for the Union.

The North had to fight for the preservation of the Union. Without the South what remained of the United States would have conceivably disintegrated. It certainly would not have become a world power.

As for slavery, had the South not seceded, slavery would have been alive and well with no interference from the North, but only for a short period. Economically, slavery was on the verge of becoming an unprofitable enterprise in 1860 and would likely have become untenable in the next few years.[121] Had it even partially survived, in some form, the evolution of Christianity and the inventions of John Deere would have quickly put an end to it.

---

[120] Sophocleus, "Emancipation Proclamation Sesquicentennial," pp. 14-15
[121] King, "Lee and Jackson Were Great Americans," pp. 6-7

VII. BLACK AND BLUE

IN AN OLD MOVIE ENTITLED "Little Big Man," an elderly Indian chieftain described the "Civil War" as "the war to free the black man." Through countless similar references in the entertainment industry and through misguided or incompetent teachers using textbooks revised by omission, the chief's viewpoint has become ingrained in our society.

A few who took up arms on the Union side were indeed abolitionists. Ninety percent were not. Then there were the "copperheads" in the North who supported the South's right to secede. They refused to take up arms to fight the Confederacy.[122] Through the letters and diaries of the common Union soldier and the actions, statements, and reports of their superior officers, it is clear that a vast majority had no concern for the ideology of abolition, and indeed some, if not most, held the Negro in utter contempt. The preservation of the Union was by far the strongest incentive to fight for the "boys in blue."

Hayward Morton, a soldier with the famed 7th Massachusetts Volunteer Infantry, wrote home in 1862: "The men are sick of war... [and] are down on the abolitionists and

---

[122] Bell Irving Wiley, *They Who Fought Here*, Bonanza Books, 1959, pp. 4, 8-11, 16-19, 173-174, 194

43

will give them particular fits when they get home again. There is no love of your nigger men here in the army. We all hate the sight of a nigger worse than a snake, and when we are on the march and come across any of them, they call them all manner of names and throw stones and sticks at them. In fact, anything is not too bad for anyone of the damned niggers, as the boys call them."[123]

Private Robert Goodyear of the 27th Connecticut describes a scene at Falmouth, Virginia, where he and his unit were guarding an ammo train, that typifies the lack of empathy among Union soldiers for blacks. Several white civilians walked into their midst, tied a Negro to a beam and applied six lashes to his back. No Union soldiers interfered and Private Goodyear described the event as a "slight interruption" to his letter writing. It is further enlightening to see that subsequently he wrote, "I fight so our Great Government may be preserved from treason and anarchy."[124]

That was virtually the sole sentiment of the brigades and regiments of Union soldiers of foreign birth. They were especially patriotic because most had come to America to escape just such division in the homelands. The hardships that such discord had created prompted them to prevent such from happening in their new "promised land."[125] There were, of course, a great number (especially Irish), who had no

[123] Tapert, *The Brother's War*, pp. 99, 117, 130-131, 137, 191, 210-212, 229
[124] *Ibid.*
[125] Wiley, *They Who Fought Here*, pp. 4, 8-11, 16-19, 173-174, 194

opportunity to consider fidelity since they were automatically drafted into Union service as soon as they stepped off of the boat.

The Union soldiers who held no particular views on slavery were nonetheless at best crass and condescending in their attitudes toward slaves. At worst, they looked upon slaves as contemptible. Lt. Samuel Nichols of the 37th Massachusetts wrote home to his family: "Ask father if he would not like to have a darky work for him when I come home. I presume I might bring one home. It is sport to have them around."[126]

Many Union soldiers, especially from the border states, owned slaves. Certainly, they were not fighting for their emancipation. Nor were those from Northern states which had passed "Exclusion Laws" to prevent the immigration of blacks into their borders.[127] These Union soldiers feared that freed blacks would inundate their towns and cities and they did not want to be near them.[128]

Others, like Eugene McWayne of Illinois, cared not for their freedom and were only interested in their entertainment value. He had to march all the way to Georgia to see his "first full blooded African." At his post on a captured plantation, Private McWayne was enthralled to see that they could "pat, sing and dance at the same time." He wrote, "It is worth more

---

[126] Tapert, *The Brother's War*, pp. 99, 117, 130-131, 137, 191, 210-212, 229
[127] Marksburg, "Culture Wars and Revisionist History," pp. 20, 26-29
[128] Davison, State of Alabama Senate Speech

to see them than all the theaters or circuses in the whole north."[129]

Other Union soldiers held no such benign dispositions. There are astonishingly numerous instances of Northern miscreants abusing Negroes. Union authorities reported that the "rogues" ransacked Negro cabins and despoiled the occupants of their meager possessions. One of Grant's officers said, during the Vicksburg campaign: "God knows, the infantry is bad enough. The damn thieves even steal from the Negroes."[130]

Union generals were often no less culpable than the soldiers they commanded. In Mississippi, "liberated" slaves were not set free, but were forced to continue working on captured plantations to provide free cotton to the Northern factories. And, Union generals offered to help the governors of the border states to "put down with an iron hand" any slave insurrections that might occur. Further, Union troops were employed as slave catchers for runaways in those states.[131]

Grant, Sherman and most other Union generals opposed freed Negroes from remaining in or about their camps. Such refugees followed Federal units by the hundreds and sometimes thousands, clinging close for the only sustenance and protection they had. This caused major logistic and

---

[129] Tapert, *The Brother's War*, pp. 99, 117, 130-131, 137, 191, 210-212, 229
[130] Wiley, *They Who Fought Here*, pp. 4, 8-11, 16-19, 173-174, 194
[131] Davison, State of Alabama Senate Speech

strategy problems in that Sherman's forces were dependent upon foraging for food for themselves in hostile territory and troop movements were hindered by the "hangers-on."[132]

In his famous march through Georgia, Sherman had pontoon bridges built across Ebenezer Creek. When all his soldiers had crossed, he had the bridges cutaway, stranding the blacks and leaving them to fend for themselves.[133] Sherman described black refugees as "useless mouths to feed" and "a dead weight on me."[134] Sherman's lack of sympathy for the plight of the blacks was also evident in his approach to solving the problem of protecting his soldiers from landmines. He simply had the blacks walk the Georgia roads in front of his troop columns.

U.S. generals also opposed black people remaining about their camps out of concern for the rampant prostitution among the "colored women." Their concerns were that such would affect both the "health and morality" of their soldiers.[135] Demonstrating that point, a Maine regiment complained they had nothing to amuse themselves with "except little nigger wenches."[136]

---

[132] Wiley, *They Who Fought Here*, pp. 4, 8-11, 16-19, 173-174, 194
[133] Zwemer, *Civil War Trivia*, pp. 54, 58, 61, 111, 103-104
[134] Davis and Wiley, *Civil War – A Complete Photographic History*, pp. 8, 370-376, 382, 430, 578, 815, 888
[135] Wiley, *They Who Fought Here*, pp. 4, 8-11, 16-19, 173-174, 194
[136] *Ibid.*

A large majority of young Northern civilians were even less enamored with the fate of the Negro, abolition, or even patriotism for the United States. Of the 170,000 conscripts (draftees) in the North, 120,000 paid substitutes to take their places in the ranks. That practice by the way, was a perfectly legal alternative to military service.[137]

So adamant were they in their reluctance to fight in what they increasingly perceived was a conflict over slavery after the issuance of the Emancipation Proclamation, New Yorkers went on a rampage in 1863. Over 1,000 were killed and many thousands were injured in what became known as the "Draft Riots."[138]. A dozen black freedmen were lynched. Any seen on the street were beaten and tortured. Fifty public buildings, two churches and a black orphanage were burned to the ground over a period of three days. Blacks fled the city by the thousands and their New York population dropped lower than it had been in over 40 years.

There is scant evidence of any concern among Northern soldiers or a majority of civilians about slaves or slavery. A Federal in blue and a Confederate in gray, wounded at Cedar Mountain in 1862, found themselves alone and unarmed in a barn on that battlefield. In the ensuing conversation, the Reb

---

[137] *Ibid.*

[138] Benson J. Lossing, *Matthew Brady's Illustrated History Of The Civil War*, Fairfax Press, 1912, pp. 6, 256

asked the Yank, "Why did you come down here fighting us? The Yank replied, "For the old flag."[139] That sums it up well.

---

[139] Wiley, *They Who Fought Here*, pp. 4, 8-11, 16-19, 173-174, 194

VIII. Black in Gray

IT IS COMMON "KNOWLEDGE" that blacks neither supported nor fought for the South. That common knowledge is wrong. The Confederate army was a diverse group.[140] Besides the three brigades of Native Americans and the 5-10 % of Confederate soldiers who were of foreign birth and the untold tens of thousands of "Yankees" from Northern states,[141] black freedmen and even slaves picked up arms to defend the South.

Though neither Confederate nor Union forces accepted black volunteers at the beginning of the War, there were a number of Confederates who were "possessed of enough Negro blood to merit classification by law as colored," who were full- fledged combatants and fought in many engagements for the South from the beginning.[142] Most were mulattoes or light-skinned, but they did indeed wear the gray.

Dick Langhorne, a black soldier of the 11th Virginia Infantry, was the first freedman to receive a medal of commendation. And he did so in the first major battle of the War, First

---

[140] *Ibid.*
[141] Wiley, *Embattled Confederates*, pp. 6, 65, 77, 191-192, 231-238, 240-244, 247
[142] Wiley, *They Who Fought Here*, pp. 4, 8-11, 16-19, 173-174, 194

Manassas. The award was granted for taking Union prisoners.[143]

Thousands of blacks, both free and slave, served the Confederacy as members of the state militias, they fulfilled provost duties, guarded prisoners, relayed information on troop movements, and served as a "first line of defense" for towns and cities. Many served in the small Confederate Navy, both free and slave (with permission from their masters).[144]

In 1861, black freedmen took it upon themselves to organize a regiment in New Orleans. They never saw action and eventually disbanded.[145] Assuredly, most freedmen who supported the Southern cause did so because of economics. Reflecting that notion, a free black man named Bowman Seale wrote to President Davis volunteering his services to the CSA. "If the North wins," he wrote, "the best poor man's country in the world will very soon be converted into a land of the extremist want and misery."[146] (His prediction was absolutely correct.)

Most freedmen who participated on behalf of the South did not do so in combat. They served as paid teamsters, railroad men, barge captains and in other vital and consequential occupations.[147] (38) A great majority of blacks who worked for

---

[143] Napier, "Warriors"
[144] Barrows, Segars, and Rosenburg, *Forgotten Confederates*
[145] Wiley, *Embattled Confederates*, pp. 6, 65, 77, 191-192, 231-238, 240-244, 247
[146] Napier, "Warriors"
[147] Wiley, *They Who Fought Here*, pp. 4, 8-11, 16-19, 173-174, 194

the South were slaves used as laborers to construct roads and fortifications.[148]   Slaves who were brought to war with their masters (and these were in considerable numbers), most often proved not only their fidelity, but their courage.

There are many documented instances of these "body servants" standing guard duty, serving as snipers, and voluntarily going into the battle lines. There are a plethora of photos showing blacks in Confederate encampments, some armed. They sought out and brought wounded Confederate soldiers from the battlefield, often in the very midst of battle and carnage and at great personal risk.

In 1864, one such slave proclaimed his loyalty to the Southern cause in a letter he wrote to Richard Will, brother of the recently slain Lt. George Will of the 42nd North Carolina. It was a poignant communication relating to the soldier's demise and ending with, "I am willing to do anything to help out our struggling country...Master Richard, I know something about trouble. Your faithful servant, Wash."[149]

With few exceptions, the CSA had no organization of regular army black troops until 1865. The Confederate Congress finally authorized the mustering of 300,000 to serve the Confederacy, an act for which Robert E. Lee had been begging for two years.[150]   Early that year, the citizens of

---

[148] Wiley, *Embattled Confederates*, pp. 6, 65, 77, 191-192, 231-238, 240-244, 247
[149] *Ibid.*
[150] *Ibid.*

Richmond were "treated to the spectacle" of several companies of colored troops drilling in Capitol Square and wearing Confederate gray.[151] It was too little, too late. Had that act been invoked sooner, the Confederate States of America might be on modern maps.

After the War and after freedom for the slaves, there was still black support for the Southern cause. Black veterans were carried on the rolls of Confederate Veterans' organizations. There are photos of them attending Confederate reunions. Some received Confederate State pensions. Twenty years after the War, James and Anna Hale, a black couple in Montgomery, were among the leading contributors to the Alabama Confederate Soldiers Monument in that city. [152]

In 1890, 25 years after the War, a Republican from Washington County, Mississippi, named John F. Harris, in a bid to raise a monument for the Confederate dead, gave a speech to the State Legislature. "When news came that the South had been invaded, our men went forth to fight for their country and what they believed and they made no requests for monuments. But they died and their virtues should be remembered. Mr. Speaker, I went with them. I, too, wore the gray…We stayed for four long years and if that war had gone on until now, I would have been there yet."

---

[151] *Ibid.*; Phillip Van Doren Stern, *Robert E. Lee*, Bonanza Books, 1969, pp. 199-200

[152] Napier, "Warriors"

Mr. Harris had been a slave and went to war with his master.

IX. BLACK IN BLUE

IN THE FIRST TWO YEARS of the War, there were several Negroes who could pass for white that enlisted in the Union army. When their racial identity was discovered, they were summarily discharged. Eventually, black units, led by white officers but otherwise segregated from white soldiers, were formed and thousand of blacks wore Federal blue.

However, almost all were restricted to labor companies or garrison duty and were little more than uniformed drudges.[153] Further, black soldiers received only half the pay of their white counterparts; were issued inferior equipment; shorted on clothing and often on rations.

Hollywood's movie *Glory* left the impression that black soldiers were used extensively in combat. They were not. To the entertainment industry's credit, the climactic battle in which they were engaged realistically portrayed their decimation and utter defeat.[154] However, the film glossed over the fact that the unit was purposefully used as cannon fodder in a frontal attack over open ground upon an

---

[153] Wiley, *They Who Fought Here*, pp. 4, 8-11, 16-19, 173-174, 194
[154] James I. Robertson, Jr., *For Us the Living*, Fall River Press, 2010

unassailable fortification. Fort Wagner did not fall into Union hands until the War was over.

Another example of the use of black troops as cannon fodder is the "Battle of the Crater" at Petersburg, Virginia. In 1864, Union General Burnside ordered that mines be dug under the Confederate fortifications, filled with explosives, and ignited. The result was the immediate death of several hundred Southerners and the appearance of a huge crater, through which the Union attacked. The resulting Confederate victory was devastating for Burnside's troops and particularly for the reputation of the black units involved.

Charles Smith of the 1st Connecticut Heavy Artillery echoed the sentiments of virtually all the white soldiers in blue with the following: "We lost 3,000 men during the day, killed, wounded and missing. This was all the fault of the nigger troops, for the rebel force that opposed them was not more than one-third as large as our own. [This} disaster has completely discouraged the troops in Burnside's Corps and they say, both officers and men, that they will never fight again as long as nigger troops are with them."[155]

Black civilians, mostly newly freed slaves, who, as discussed earlier, flocked to the Union camps, also participated in non-combat roles. They were used in construction and transportation projects. But as scores of encampment photos attest, they were more often utilized for

---

[155] Tapert, *The Brother's War*, pp. 99, 117, 130-131, 137, 191, 210-212, 229

menial domestic labor by individual soldiers, most often officers. An unknown non-commissioned officer wrote: "I have a little nigger to wait on me and am growing quite corpulent. How much easier it is to have a little nig to take your extra steps."[156]

Another letter, written by Lt. John Sturtevant of New Hampshire, reflects the lack of dignity Union troops afforded the black race: "My colored man I don't think I can get along without." After describing his duties as a valet and cook, the lieutenant continued with, "I did not like the name of 'Jim" for my boy, so I changed his name to 'Eldridge' in honor of the grocery store man."[157]

There was little respect, regard or consideration for blacks by soldiers of the United States Army.

[156] Wiley, *They Who Fought Here*, pp. 4, 8-11, 16-19, 173-174, 194
[157] Tapert, *The Brother's War*, pp. 99, 117, 130-131, 137, 191, 210-212, 229

X. THE BLACK AND WHITE
THAT ISN'T

BLACK AND WHITE. Right and wrong. Good and evil. That is the way we like to perceive things. It is simple and easy. No need for all those pesky inconsistencies, awkward incongruities and doubtful evaluations.

But the black and white of the War is non-existent. From the fact that several counties in north Alabama tried to secede from the state during the War to the fact that Mary Todd Lincoln's two half-brothers and two brothers-in-law fought for the Confederacy, definitive lines simply cannot be drawn.[158] From the fact that Confederate General Stonewall Jackson opposed slavery and secession and often prayed with blacks in Sunday school classes that he organized,[159] to the fact that the Union state of Delaware was the last state in America to free its slaves after the War, there is little that can be classified as categorical.

Confederate President Jefferson Davis and his wife heard of a black orphan named Jim Limber who had been placed with

---

[158] Jordan, *The Civil War*, pp. 11-13, 18, 27, 30, 32-33, 112
[159] *Ibid*.

a black family living near their residence. The rumor was that the child was being badly mistreated. Mrs. Davis took the time and effort in the middle of the War to investigate. She took Jim to their home, had his wounds doctored, and he was welcomed into the Confederate White House. President Davis personally registered his "free papers." Shortly before Richmond fell President Davis went to an attorney and made arrangements to secure Jim's future education.[160]

Confederate General Robert E. Lee, whom Winston Churchill called "the most noble American who ever lived,"[161] and Franklin D. Roosevelt called "one of the greatest American Christians,"[162] and of whom Dwight D. Eisenhower said, "A nation of men of Lee's caliber would be unconquerable in both soul and spirit"[163] was against both secession and slavery.[164] Seven years before the War, he wrote to his wife, "Slavery as an institution is a moral and political evil in any country."[165] After the War, in which he had fought so brilliantly and valiantly, he said, "So far as engaging in a war to perpetuate slavery, I am rejoiced that slavery is

[160] Davison, State of Alabama Senate Speech
[161] King, "Lee and Jackson Were Great Americans," pp. 6-7
[162] *Ibid.*
[163] *Ibid.*
[164] Phillip Van Doren Stern, *Robert E. Lee*, pp. 199-200
[165] Robert E. Lee, "Quotes About Slavery," AZ Quotes, https://www.azquotes.com/author/8660-Robert_E_Lee/tag/slavery

abolished. I would have cheerfully lost all that I have to have this attained."[166]

Your history teacher probably didn't mention this when discussing the two most prominent leaders of the Confederacy. Nor did he or she probably mention the fact that Abraham Lincoln desecrated the U.S. Constitution when he suspended Writ of Habeas Corpus in the North.[167] He imprisoned up to 200,000 Union citizens (38,000 for the duration of the War) without warrant or trial for opposing the invasion of the South. He had his troops shut down over 300 newspapers and burn many of them for editorializing against his politics. Many civilians in St. Louis and Baltimore were killed and dozens wounded for protesting the War.[168] Lincoln placed 50 cannon around Baltimore with direct orders to bombard it if resistance continued.[169]

Nor did they probably mention that Union General Ulysses S. Grant was a slave owner. Grant was the eighth general appointed by Lincoln in his desperate attempt to find someone who could "whip Bobby Lee."[170] Though the North had greatly superior arms, equipment, and numbers, Grant was primarily successful because of his lack of concern for his own

---

[166] *Ibid.*

[167] John M. Taylor, "Tyranny in Maryland," *Alabama Confederate*, Apr 2016, pp. 24-25

[168] *Ibid.*

[169] *Ibid.*

[170] "Abraham Lincoln – An Illustrated History of His Life and Times," pp. 58-61, 88-89, 94

troops. The North lost over 100,000 more men than the South. Grant never apologized for the slaughter into which he sent his troops at Cold Harbor. The defeat of Lee was of much more import than the welfare of his own men.

You probably didn't hear in the classroom that both Lincoln and Grant supported the concept of "total war," most widely practiced by Union Generals Sherman, Sheridan and Merritt.[171] It was a military exercise by which all civilian infrastructure was utterly destroyed, including food, homes, businesses, churches, transportation systems, and schools. Livestock was stolen or killed, crops were stolen or burned and non-military industries were demolished.

In three days in the Shenandoah Valley, Merritt set ablaze 630 barns, 47 flour mills, 4 sawmills, 1 woolen mill, 3 iron furnaces, 4,000 tons of hay, 500,000 bushels of wheat and oats, 515 acres of corn, 560 barrels of flour, and drove off 3,300 head of livestock. This was a minor incursion.[172] Imagine what happened in Sherman's march through Georgia.[173] The damage in a multi-month-long campaign through a 70-mile-wide swath of utter destruction could never be estimated.[174] Sherman's march is celebrated as a great military achievement.

---

[171] Lt. Col. Joseph Mitchell, *Decisive Battles of The Civil War*, Fawcett Publications, 1955, pp. 95, 97

[172] Ken Poole, "Dispatches from the Front," *Confederate Veteran*, Mar/Apr 2016, pp. 7, 52

[173] Jordan, *The Civil War*, pp. 11-13, 18, 27, 30, 32-33, 112

[174] Wiley, *Embattled Confederates*, pp. 6, 65, 77, 191-192, 231-238, 240-244, 247

Actually, it was an almost unopposed terror campaign against civilians.

By contrast, Lee's invasion of Pennsylvania, a tactic late in the War which was designed to force the Union to consider peace, resulted only in the burning of the Caledonia Iron Works, which was designated as a military installation.[175] During this deployment, three roll calls per day were held to account for Confederate troops and ensure that there was no plundering or theft of civilian property. Lee's General Order #73 reads: "No greater disgrace could befall the army than the perpetration of the barbarous outrages upon the unarmed and defenseless and the wanton destruction of private property *that have marked the course of the enemy in our own country.*"[176]

Lee's indictment of the behavior of the Union armies in the South was well founded. Hundreds of Southern churches were burned and their cemeteries desecrated. In one South Carolina town, Union troops dug up caskets and propped them up to "watch" the church in flames. Pillage and plunder was, in some Federal units, the order of the day.[177] And civilian welfare was of little concern to invading Northern forces. It is conservatively estimated that 35,000 innocent Southern civilians died during the War.[178] (Experts continue

---

[175] Poole, "Dispatches from the Front," pp. 7, 52

[176] Kennedy, "Sharecropping and Northern Imposed Postwar Slavery," pp. 11, 16-19, 56-63 (Italics mine.)

[177] Charles Jennings, *Cultures in Conflict: The Union Desecration Of Southern Churches and Cemeteries*, Truth in History, 2001

[178] Poole, "Dispatches from the Front," pp. 7, 52

to raise this figure greatly upward.) One civilian was killed by a stray bullet in Gettysburg during Lee's invasion of the North.[179]

It was a war of dichotomies. In the Battle of Vicksburg, 22 units from Missouri fought for the Union and 17 units from Missouri fought for the Confederacy.[180] In the middle of the War, West Virginia seceded from secessionist Virginia to join the Union. The First Maryland infantry from that Union state fought for the South. Thousands of families disintegrated as members took up arms on opposing sides. "The Brother's War" was certainly not black and white.[181]

In the Battle of Cold Harbor, mentioned earlier, Grant lost 7,000 men in less than 30 minutes attacking Lee's fortifications.[182] That grim statistic is an American history record for the largest number of casualties in the shortest span of time in any war we have ever fought. After watching the slaughter of their comrades in the first wave, the second wave wrote their names and where their bodies were to be shipped on pieces of paper and pinned them to their haversacks. They too, then charged and died. They were fighting to preserve the Union and uphold their honor. It is asinine to think they went to certain death to free the slaves.

---

[179] Zwemer, *Civil War Trivia*, pp. 54, 58, 61, 111, 103-104
[180] Jordan, *The Civil War*, pp. 11-13, 18, 27, 30, 32-33, 112
[181] Tapert, *The Brother's War*, pp. 99, 117, 130-131, 137, 191, 210-212, 229
[182] Zwemer, *Civil War Trivia*, pp. 54, 58, 61, 111, 103-104

Likewise, and from the same sources of correspondence, it is intellectual simplicity to even consider that the vast majority of Confederate soldiers died to preserve an institution in which they had no interest, philosophically or economically. Three-fourths did not own slaves.[183]   They were fighting against Union tyranny and the greed and power of despotism. They were fighting for the rights of the states to govern themselves. They were fighting to protect their homes and families.

Colonel Bartleson of the 100th Illinois Infantry said it well. "We are fighting for a Union, a sentiment, a high and noble sentiment, but after all, just a sentiment. They are fighting for independence and a hatred against invaders."[184]   Only an infinitesimal few were fighting to free the slaves or maintain the institution of slavery. The War was not about slavery.

---

[183] Jordan, *The Civil War*, pp. 11-13, 18, 27, 30, 32-33, 11
[184] Tapert, *The Brother's War*, pp. 99, 117, 130-131, 137, 191, 210-212, 229

EPILOGUE

THE HISTORIC REVISION began as soon as the War ended. Napoleon said, "History is an accepted fable." And the winners of the wars write the history. Confederate General Patrick Cleburne correctly predicted, "Our youth will be trained by Northern school teachers; will learn from Northern school books their version of the war ...to regard our dead as traitors and our veterans as fit subjects for derision."[185]

Post-War indoctrination by federal authorities was quick, intentional and insidious. Brown University President Wayland said the South was "the new missionary ground for the national school teacher."[186] Howard University President Hill said it was the North's aim to "spread knowledge and culture over a region that has sat in darkness."[187] Senator Charles Sumner of Massachusetts said it was the mission of his state to govern Georgia "better than Georgia could."[188] The

---

[185] Gen. Patrick Cleburne, "Confederate Quotes" American Revival, http://www.americanrevival.org/quotes/confederate.htm

[186] John Taylor, "The Cost of Seeking Independence," *Alabama Confederate*, July 2015, pp. 7-8

[187] *Ibid.*

[188] Root, "Admiral Semmes and Those People," pp. 22, 26

same people whose arrogance and assumed superiority helped fuel secession were now dictating history.

And it has never stopped. Many contemporary histories of the "Civil War" are so obviously biased in their contemptuous presentations of the South and the Southern cause as to be laughable, were it not so sad. That is why today, our school children have never heard of the Union League, the "enforcement" arm of the Freedman's Bureau. It has been omitted from the history books because it is inconvenient to the narrative of the revisionists.

The Freedman's Bureau failed miserably in their attempts to care for newly freed blacks.[189] The Southern blacks had been plunged into abject poverty. They had no land, no jobs and no provisions. The Bureau never even came close to providing the food, clothing, shelter and medical care given to the slaves by their masters.[190] Seizing upon that failure, white "carpetbaggers" organized and controlled the Union League.

They were a secret society, supposedly involved in the indoctrination of the ex-slave to bring them into the Republican voting network, but in reality they were using the blacks to punish and exterminate ex-Confederates and gain control of their land and property. The League burned the houses and fields of whites, shot their livestock, poisoned their

[189] Kirkpatrick Sale, "Reconstruction—What Might Have Been," *Confederate Veteran*, May/Jun 2016, pp. 20-21
[190] *Ibid.*

wells and murdered their families. They attacked, tortured and killed blacks who were considered sympathetic to or who associated with whites.[191]

The depredations of the Union League and the tyrannical rule of the occupying Federal military, who gave support to carpetbaggers and who appointed unqualified blacks and corrupt Northern civilians to political posts and judgeships, gave rise to the Ku Klux Klan. This group was formed to protect Southerners besieged by these invaders.

Children today are taught that Nathan Bedford Forrest was the head of the Ku Klux Klan, but the facts simply do not support this. Dr. Michael Bradley, in a lengthy article in *Confederate Veteran Magazine* goes into great detail on this subject.[192] Children are also taught that Southerners were blatantly racist. The fact is that the vast majority of all Americans at that time were what is now termed racist. A great example of this is the following quote by Abraham Lincoln:

> I will say, then, that I am not, nor ever have been, in favor of bringing about in any way the social and

---

[191] Phillip Leigh "Union Leagues," Abbeville Institute Blog, September 28, 2016, www.abbevilleinstitute.org/blog/union-leagues

[192] Dr. Michael R. Bradley, Confederate Veteran: Volume 71, No.4, July/August, 2013

political equality of the white and black races-that I am not, nor ever have been, in favor of making voters or jurors of negroes, nor of qualifying them to hold office…[193]

Those who bandy about words such as 'racist' or 'white supremacist' are serving an agenda rather than pursuing facts. Though hated by many blacks today, Forrest was admired and trusted by blacks during his lifetime. He was invited to address the Independent Order of Pole-Bearers Association, an early black civic organization, and here are some of the words he had to say:

We were born on the same soil, breathe the same air, and live in the same land. Why, then, can we not live as brothers?

I came here with the jeers of some white people, who think that I am doing wrong. I believe that I can exert some influence, and do much to assist the people in strengthening fraternal relations, and shall do all in my power to bring about peace. It has always been my motto to elevate every man—to depress none. I want to elevate you to take positions in law offices, in stores, on farms, and wherever you are capable of going….

---

[193] Kennedy, Walter Donald, Rekilling Lincoln, Gretna, LA:Pelican Publishing, 2015, pg.56

I came to meet you as friends, and welcome you to the white people. I want you to come nearer to us. When I can serve you I will do so. We have but one flag, one country; let us stand together. We may differ in color, but not in sentiment...

Go to work, be industrious, live honestly and act truly, and when you are oppressed I'll come to your relief. I thank you, ladies and gentlemen, for this opportunity you have afforded me to be with you, and to assure you that I am with you in heart and in hand.[194]

Today students are not told that Forrest held meetings with and worked with blacks to protect their interests and improve their communities.[195] He made a point of hiring blacks and helping them succeed. Using him as a symbol of hate only serves the agenda of those attacking Southern heritage. Forrest denied any role in the founding or leadership of the KKK in Congressional testimony. The fact is that Forrest took out ads in Memphis and Nashville newspapers to encourage the disbanding of the KKK because it had "threatened to

[194] Wikisource.org, Nathan Bedford Forrest, Pole-Bearers Speech

[195] Kennedy, "Sharecropping and Northern Imposed Postwar Slavery," pp. 11, 16-19, 56-63

degenerate into an instrument of personal vengeance."[196] Children today are not told that the original KKK ceased when the occupiers left. They are not told that the later white supremacist groups commandeered their name and have nothing in common with them.

The teachings of revised history would have us believe that Reconstruction was a post-war attempt by the North to revive the South. Nothing could be further from the truth. It was first of all a vast looting of Southern wealth by Northerners. And it was forced acculturation to Northern beliefs and social systems.[197] Reeducation was the key component of this notion. It had nothing to do with the physical reconstruction in terms of infrastructure, which was destroyed with the Union practice of "total war."[198]

Not only was the South never compensated for this purposeful devastation, but Northern political corruption and outright theft in the South after the War continued to deplete and destroy the economy. One hundred years after the War, not one Southern state was in the top 50% of national per capita income.[199] Five years after the end of the War, General

---

[196] Wiley, *Embattled Confederates*, pp. 6, 65, 77, 191-192, 231-238, 240-244, 247

[197] Marksburg, "Culture Wars and Revisionist History," pp. 20, 26-29
[198] Sale, "Reconstruction — What Might Have Been," pp. 20-21
[199] Taylor, "The Cost of Seeking Independence," pp. 7-8

Lee told Governor Stockdale that he would have never surrendered had he known the oppression that would be instituted against the South.[200]

General Cleburne's prognostications were correct. The scape-goating of the Confederacy was swift and vicious. Of typical example, the painting of Southerners as animalistic brutes was showcased in the Northern description of Andersonville Prison. The Confederate government and army was accused of deliberate and sadistic mistreatment of Union prisoners at that facility. The Warden, Major Henry Wirz, was put on trial, found guilty and hanged.[201] The truth of the matter was totally ignored.

In 1864 the Confederacy was barely able to feed and equip its own soldiers. The Andersonville authorities begged the Union for a prisoner exchange to alleviate the suffering and starvation of the Union captives. The U.S. government refused the exchange. Grant said it was cheaper to feed Confederate prisoners than to fight them. They knew full well the South was incapable of properly caring for the prisoners, but ignored their pleas.[202]

---

[200] *Ibid.*

[201] Davis and Wiley, *Civil War – A Complete Photographic History*, pp. 8, 370-376, 382, 430, 578, 815, 888

[202] Karen Stokes, "An Unrighteous and Diabolical War," *Confederate Veteran*, Mar/Apr 2016, pp. 17-18

Then Confederate Commissioner Colonel Ould offered to return the Union prisoners at Andersonville without exchange in the summer of 1864, just to save their lives. Lincoln and the Union authorities disregarded that offer for a full six months. That was the period in which most of the Union deaths at the prison occurred.[203] Indeed, history is an accepted fable.

The Union hubris and hypocrisy of this sorry matter is exacerbated by the fact that Confederate prisoners were deliberately abused, mistreated and many murdered in Union prisons, even though the North had plentiful supplies. In places like Camp Douglas, Elmira, Morris Island, the Confederates were placed on starvation diets with rancid water, and denied clothing, blankets and heat in freezing weather. On the prison ship "Crescent City," they were locked in the hold for weeks without fresh air, light or sanitation facilities.[204] This is not mentioned in mainstream revised history.

This reeducation also, in an attempt to further the Union agenda, completely overlooked Northern support for the South. Hundreds of prominent, rich Northern industrialists were complicit in the practice of slavery and were financially dependent upon it, and not only through trade. Many of them owned slaves, especially on the rice and sugar plantations of

---

[203] *Ibid.*

[204] Joann C. Moore "Colonel Van H. Manning," *Confederate Veteran*, Jan/Feb 2017, pp. 58-66

Louisiana, Mississippi, and Cuba.[205] But following the War, the historical revisionists had begun to believe their own propaganda, especially as espoused by the puffery of the Emancipation Proclamation. By 1931, this reeducation was so deep that author H.L. Mencken declared that "Lincoln has become a national deity and a realistic examination of him is no longer possible."[206]

It is difficult to say whether Lincoln, who supported the "total war" policy of his generals, resulting in the economic and physical ruin of the South, would have actually acted upon his "with malice toward none" promise in his Second Inaugural Address. After all, he had said in his First Inaugural Address: "The lawless invasion by armed force of the soil of any state or territory, no matter under what pretext, is among the gravest of crimes."[207] Then a few weeks later, he invaded the South. It is doubtful the South would have fared any better under his continued Presidency, but John Wilkes Booth assured us we will never know.

We do know that the subsequent government, in its zest for retribution, revenge and retaliation, plunged the South into a hell in which it suffered for more than 100 years, and in some

----

[205] Kennedy, "Sharecropping and Northern Imposed Postwar Slavery," pp. 11, 16-19, 56-63

[206] Sophocleus, "Emancipation Proclamation Sesquicentennial," pp. 14-15

[207] Loy Mauch, "What Our Confederate Ancestors Were Fighting to Save," *Confederate Veteran*, Jul/Aug 2017, p. 23

senses, is still suffering. And the venal editing of its history has guaranteed that the Southern white Christian Male is a member of the most maligned, ridiculed and misjudged geopolitical and socio-economic group in America. But that is another book.

A very wise and talented artist once told me: "The hardest part of painting is to know when you are finished."

RED, WHITE, AND BLUE: AN ESSAY

IT IS CURRENTLY POPULAR in American culture to denigrate the Confederacy, anyone who has ancestors connected to the Confederacy, the icons and symbols which represent it, and Southerners and Southern states in general. And it did not begin recently. There is a long history of hatred for the South. Even before the War, greedy Northerners, in an effort to reap financial benefits from the economically subdued agrarian states, began to paint its people as vastly inferior. "Subhuman," "agents of Satan," "animals," and "vermin" are but a few of the expletives politicians, preachers, and newspapers spewed forth. The *New York Times* wrote, "Better to kill every last man, woman and child in the South than let them get away with secession." The sentiment continues to this day.

It is my sincere hope that the facts and information contained in *Slavery and the Civil War* will be useful in combating the misinformation and fabrication so haphazardly and viciously strewn forth by those who wish to equate the Confederacy with racial hatred and bigotry and those who wish to convince themselves they are morally superior to everyone else. I pray this book is intellectual ammunition for counterattack. It has become the epitome of "political correctness" to denounce anyone and anything connected with the rebellion as the antithesis of harmonic civilization. Beware political correctness.

It was originally a propaganda tool created in the Communist reeducation camps of the mid-20th century. It manifests itself in the control of language, giving power to those who insist upon its use. Language affects thought. Thought affects action. Action results in command. It has been adopted by modern socialists and their media spokespersons to divide society and denigrate those with whom they disagree. Without such division, they cannot establish the authoritarianism necessary for ultimate totalitarian rule. Every such government in modern history, be it begun by Lenin or Stalin, Hitler or Mussolini, Mao Tse Tung, Castro, or Idi Amin, has used social division and eradication of the resulting minority to achieve its goal.

Understand that genocide is not the only means to silence dissenters. The same ends can be achieved by quieting those who disagree through ridicule, harassment and social banishment and even threats of such, if the social fabric is weak, as ours is today. It works just as well as firing squads and death camps. You need go no further than this book to view the insidious nature of political correctness. The man who wrote the original introduction to this work is an attorney who was in private practice at the time. He has since been appointed to a position with the government. When the publication of *Slavery and the Civil War* became imminent, he asked that his contribution and his name be removed from it because his current employers would fire him if it were discovered he was associated with such a politically incorrect book. Think of it. The mere association with truth or anything contrary to modern Orwellian "group- think" is reason for contempt and the destruction of a career.

Those who wish to divide us prey upon the misinformed, the ill-informed, the uninformed, and the ignorant. They use half-truths, innuendos, altered statistics, outright lies, and blatant omissions. The only way to combat this assault is with veracity. And that must be presented at every opportunity. Anyone interested in preserving dignity, heritage and history needs to respond with facts whenever they hear or read anything contrary to the truth. People who, for whatever reason, wish to demonize those who respect Southern heritage cannot stand up to the light of truth.

For instance, it can be readily pointed out that those who have recently called for the destruction of the relief carvings of Confederates on Stone Mountain in Georgia, are using the same tactics as the Taliban, who dynamited old carvings of Buddha in Afghanistan. People who blow up rocks with which they disagree are a psychotic and dangerous lot.

These people and their allies base their "righteous indignation" on three baseless concepts. (1) The Confederacy seceded to maintain slavery. (2) Slavery is racism. (3) Contemporary White supremacist groups began in the Confederacy, as proven by their use of the Confederate flag. This book is replete with information to thoroughly disprove these allegations.

For instance, the very ugly and twisted specter of "reparations" has raised its progressive head yet once again.

In this age of perpetual victimization, it is little wonder. How simple it is to refute using the information in this book. Whites owned Black and White slaves. A huge majority of Whites never owned any slaves. American Indians owned White, Black and American Indian slaves. Blacks owned Black slaves and it was Blacks who sold Black slaves into slavery to begin with. Most Americans did not come here until after the 13th amendment was ratified. If "reparation" is to work, we have to determine who will pay whom. How will culpability and entitlements be determined?

The proponents of "reparations" cannot answer that question. And they are incapable of embarrassment, but we can ask it anyway. The inaptly named "social justice" movement are the instigators of this silly notion. They consist of Marxist politicians and their radical allies who wish to perpetuate their power and their paychecks; exploit the naïve and uninformed; and adhere to the communist principle of wealth redistribution. Social justice has nothing to do with it and apparently, neither does history. In 20th century Europe and Asia, the masters of tens of millions of slaves were the same race as the slaves themselves. Slavery is an economic institution. It is not racist. It is opportunistic. Just as it was in the 19th century.

AFTERWORD

AS OF LATE, the Confederate flag has been the target of the myth purveyors. They need to be reminded that white supremacist groups (which, as noted in this work, the original KKK was not) also use the American flag and the Christian cross as their symbols. And there is no hue and cry to have those icons removed from public view. Extremist groups can use or misuse whatever symbol they wish. It does not make the symbol evil. They need to be reminded that no slave ship ever flew a Confederate flag. Those ships sailed under the standards of the United States of America and several European countries. If they want a flag to hate, it should be that of Nigeria or other African countries who sold their own people into slavery.

But the progressives, socialists and communists and their professional victims and their allies in the media, the entertainment industry, the halls of academia and the cowardly politicians who fear them want every vestige of the Confederacy destroyed. And they want to make heroes out of Union leaders. Our kids today are being taught that Abraham Lincoln is a national hero. He was many things, but "hero" is not one of them. As demonstrated in this book, he was a Domestic Terrorist, a War Criminal, a White Supremacist, and an Anti-Constitutionalist. He was also the worst commander-in-chief in American History. Many of his generals and his own secretary of war detested him, calling him the "original gorilla." Most of all, he was a vile hypocrite and a consummate liar. Our personal favorite example of this came in his First Inaugural Address. He said there could never be a viable reason to invade a sovereign state. A few weeks later, he invaded seven of them.

If "those people" go unopposed, the flag will only be the first casualty. They are working on the statues as this is written. In New Orleans recently, the mayor and city council, against the wishes of the citizens of Louisiana, voted to remove the statues of Robert E. Lee, Jefferson Davis, and the son of their city, P.G.T. Beauregard, because they "represented racism." As discussed earlier in this work, it is apparent the first two cannot be defined as racists. And General Beauregard's credentials eliminate him completely from that title. After the War, he helped found the Reform Party, whose primary goal was to provide civil rights and voting rights for ex-slaves. But facts and truth do not matter to the "Tear 'em all down" crowd.

After the statues will be the changing of names, including streets and schools and military installations. Next will come any visual or verbal references in movies and music. Finally, will be the books (and Hitler and Lenin will be applauding from Hell), until all references to and vestiges of the Confederacy will be destroyed and history will be permanently rewritten. If we allow this, in the end we will look around and say, "My God, what have we done?"

In the early half of the last century, Mr. Frank Owsley wrote in his essay "The Irrepressible Conflict," that after the North's victory, the mind of the South and of Southerners also had to be conquered, opining that "their spirit must be invaded and destroyed; so there commenced a second war of conquest, the conquest of the Southern mind, calculated to remake every Southern opinion, to impose the Northern way of life and thought upon the South, write "error" across the pages of Southern history which were out of keeping with the Northern legend, and set the rising and unborn generations upon stools of everlasting repentance."

* * *

There is the story of a general, whose name and side change with each telling, sitting on horseback during a battle, yelling at a retreating private, "Why are you running, soldier?" Without stopping, the wild-eyed young man yelled back, "Because I can't fly!" There is always a lot of truth in humor. It is up to those of us who know the truth today to tell the truth to those who don't, which make up a majority of our society. But in the face of adversity, ridicule, and derision that inevitably arise when truth is spoken, we find it easier just to remain silent. We cannot retreat, run or fly away from our duty to reclaim our history from those who have rewritten it for their own insidious, political purposes. Robert E. Lee said, "The enemy is there and that is where we will attack.

* * *

Within five years after the War, according to the records of the Freedman's Bureau, over one million ex-slaves (almost twice the total number of casualties in the Union and Confederate armies combined) died of starvation and disease under the "care" of a myriad of Union agencies who were delegated to help them and the occupying Union army who were duty bound to protect them, proving yet again that the federal government cared not one iota about blacks. When 25% of a population perishes, it is designated as a holocaust. In their headlong rush to condemn and scapegoat the South and all things Confederate, the revisionists have chosen to ignore that fact, as well as Lincoln's response to their plight: "Root hog, or die."

BIBLIOGRAPHY

Books

Barrows, Segars, and Rosenburg, *Forgotten Confederates, An Anthology of Black Southerners*, Southern Heritage Press, 1995.

William C. Davis and Bell I. Wiley, *Civil War – A Complete Photographic History*, New York: Tess Press, 2000.

Stephen T. Foster, *Lincoln On Slavery-A Moral Wrong, But...*, Atlas Editions, n.d.

Zora Neale Hurston, *Dust Tracks On The Road*, J. B. Lippincott & Co., 1942.

Charles Jennings, *Cultures in Conflict: The Union Desecration Of Southern Churches and Cemeteries*, Truth in History, 2001.

Paul Jordan, *The Civil War*, National Geographic Society, 1969.

Benson J. Lossing, *Matthew Brady's Illustrated History of the Civil War*, Fairfax Press, 1912.

Lt. Col. Joseph Mitchell, *Decisive Battles of the Civil War*, Fawcett Publications, 1955.

Albert Pickett, *Pickett's History of Alabama*, 1851.

James I. Robertson, Jr., *For Us the Living*, Fall River Press, 2010.

Phillip Van Doren Stern, *Robert E. Lee*, Bonanza Books, 1969.

Annette Tapert, *The Brother's War*, Random House, 1988.

Bell Irving Wiley, *Embattled Confederates*, New York: Bonanza Books, 1964.

Bell Irving Wiley, *They Who Fought Here*, Bonanza Books, 1959.

John Zwemer, *Civil War Trivia*, Sweetwater Press, 2006.

Documents

"Ending Slavery in the District of Columbia," DC.gov, www.emancipation.dc.gov/page/ending-slavery-district-columbia

Thomas Jefferson, "The unanimous Declaration of the thirteen united States of America," National Archives, www.archives.gov/founding-docs/declaration-transcript

Abraham Lincoln, "Emancipation Proclamation" (1863), National Archives, www.archives.gov/exhibits/featured-documents/emancipation-proclamation/transcript.html

Articles

"Abraham Lincoln—An Illustrated History of His Life and Times," *Time Magazine*, 2009.

"America's Fascinating Indian Heritage," *Readers Digest*, 1978.

Senator Charles Davison, State of Alabama Senate Speech, Transcript, Confederate Heritage Fund, 1997.

Daniel Deville, "White Slavery in America," VN Forum, September 5, 2008, www.vnnforum.com/showthread.php?t=79466

"Indentured Servitude," Wikipedia, n.d., en.wikipedia.org/wiki/Indentured servitude

James Ronald Kennedy, "Sharecropping and Northern Imposed Postwar Slavery," *Confederate Veteran*, Jan/Feb 2016.

James W. King, "Lee and Jackson Were Great Americans," *Confederate Veteran*, Mar/Apr 2016, pp. 6-7.

Gene Kizer, Jr., "The Absurdity of Slavery as a Cause of the War," *Confederate Veteran,* Mar/Apr 2017.

Robert E. Lee, "Quotes About Slavery," AZ Quotes, www.azquotes.com/author/8660-Robert_E_Lee/tag/slavery

Phillip Leigh "Union Leagues," Abbeville Institute Blog, September 28, 2016, www.abbevilleinstitute.org/blog/union-leagues

Dan McLaughlin, "Rethinking President Grant (Part Two)," *National Review*, February 26, 2019, www.nationalreview.com/2019/02/ulysses-grant-presidency-economy-corruption-foreign-policy/

Richard Marksburg, "Culture Wars and Revisionist History," *Confederate Veteran*, Jul/Aug 2016, pp. 20, 26-29

Loy Mauch, "What Our Confederate Ancestors Were Fighting to Save," *Confederate Veteran*, Jul/Aug 2017.

Joann C. Moore "Colonel Van H. Manning," *Confederate Veteran*, Jan/Feb 2017.

Col. John Napier, "Warriors," *Capitol Confederate Newsletter*, 1996. (Reprinted from *Montgomery Advertiser*, 1861)

Dr. Ray L. Parker, "The Union Was Never in Jeopardy," *Confederate Veteran*, May/Jun 2017.

Ken Poole, "Dispatches from the Front," *Confederate Veteran*, Mar/Apr 2016.

Tom Root, "Admiral Semmes and Those People," *Confederate Veteran*, Mar/Apr 2016.

Kirkpatrick Sale, "Reconstruction — What Might Have Been," *Confederate Veteran,* May/Jun 2016.

"Slave Codes," Wikipedia, n.d., en.wikipedia.org/wiki/Slave_codes

John Sophocleus, "Emancipation Proclamation Sesquicentennial," *Alabama Gazette,* January 2013.

Karen Stokes, "An Unrighteous and Diabolical War," *Confederate Veteran*, Mar/Apr 2016.

John Taylor, "The Cost of Seeking Independence," *Alabama Confederate*, July 2015.

John M. Taylor, "Tyranny in Maryland," *Alabama Confederate*, April 2016.

John M. Taylor, "Union at All Costs," *Confederate Veteran,* Jan/Feb 2017.

ABOUT THE AUTHOR

GARRY BOWERS was for 20 years a teacher and administrator in Alabama schools. For the next 21 years he was a deputy sheriff and a writer for weekly newspapers. Since retirement he publishes regularly in outdoor magazines. He lives in Montgomery with his wife Linda. They are blessed with seven children and "too many grandchildren to count."

I would like to acknowledge and thank Tim Kent of the *Alabama Confederate* Magazine for his support and assistance with this project.

AVAILABLE FROM SHOTWELL PUBLISHING

IF YOU ENJOYED THIS BOOK, perhaps some of our other titles will pique your interest. The following titles are now available at all major online retailers. Enjoy!

JOYCE BENNETT

- *Maryland, My Maryland: The Cultural Cleansing of a Small Southern State*

JERRY BREWER

- *Dismantling the Republic*

ANDREW P. CALHOUN, JR.

- *My Own Darling Wife: Letters From a Confederate Volunteer [John Francis Calhoun]*

JOHN CHODES

- *Segregation: Federal Policy or Racism?*
- *Washington's KKK: The Union League During Southern Reconstruction*

SLAVERY AND THE CIVIL WAR

PAUL C. GRAHAM

- *Confederaphobia: An American Epidemic*
- *When the Yankees Come: Former South Carolina Slaves Remember Sherman's Invasion*

JOSEPH JAY

- *Sacred Conviction: The South's Stand for Biblical Authority*

JAMES R. KENNEDY

- *Dixie Rising: Rules for Rebels*

JAMES R. & WALTER D. KENNEDY

- *Punished with Poverty: The Suffering South*
- *Yankee Empire: Aggressive Abroad and Despotic At Home*

PHILIP LEIGH

- *The Devil's Town: Hot Spring During the Gangster Era*
- *U.S. Grant's Failed Presidency*

MICHAEL MARTIN

- *Southern Grit: Sensing the Siege at Petersburg*

LEWIS LIBERMAN

- *Snowflake Buddies: ABCs for Leftism for Kids!*

CHARLES T. PACE

- *Lincoln As He Really Was*
- *Southern Independence. Why War?*

JAMES RUTLEDGE ROESCH

- *From Founding Fathers to Fire Eaters: The Constitutional Doctrine of States' Rights in the Old South*

KIRKPATRICK SALE

- *Emancipation Hell: The Tragedy Wrought By Lincoln's Emancipation Proclamation*

KAREN STOKES

- *A Legion of Devils: Sherman in South Carolina*
- *Carolina Love Letters*

JOHN VINSON

- *Southerner, Take Your Stand!*

HOWARD RAY WHITE

- *Understanding Creation and Evolution*

CLYDE N. WILSON

- *Annals of the Stupid Party: Republicans Before Trump* (The Wilson Files 3)
- *Lies My Teacher Told Me: The True History of the War for Southern Independence*
- *Nullification: Reclaiming Consent of the Governed* (The Wilson Files 2)
- *The Old South: 50 Essential Books* (Southern Reader's Guide I)
- *The War Between the States: 60 Essential Books* (Southern Reader's Guide II)
- *The Yankee Problem: An American Dilemma* (The Wilson Files 1)

WALTER KIRK WOOD

- *Beyond Slavery: The Northern Romantic Nationalist Origins of America's Civil War*

GREEN ALTAR BOOKS (Literary/Fiction Imprint)

RANDALL IVEY

- *A New England Romance & Other SOUTHERN Stories*

JAMES EVERETT KIBLER

- *Tiller (Clay Bank County, IV)*

THOMAS MOORE

- *A Fatal Mercy: The Man Who Lost The Civil War*

KAREN STOKES

- *Belles: A Carolina Romance*
- *Honor in the Dust*
- *The Immortals*
- *The Soldier's Ghost: A Tale of Charleston*

GOLD-BUG (Mystery & Suspense Imprint)

MICHAEL ANDREW GRISSOM

- *Billie Jo*

BRANDI PERRY

- *Splintered: A New Orleans Tale*

MARTIN L. WILSON

- *To Jekyll and Hide*

FREE BOOK OFFER

SIGN-UP FOR new release notification and receive a FREE downloadable edition of *Lies My Teacher Told Me: The True History of the War for Southern Independence* by Dr. Clyde N. Wilson by visiting *FreeLiesBook.com* or by texting the word "Dixie" to 345-345. You can always unsubscribe and keep the book, so you've got nothing to lose!

Southern Without Apology

www.ingramcontent.com/pod-product-compliance
Lightning Source LLC
Chambersburg PA
CBHW070016110426
42741CB00034B/1973